bugs

By Penelope Arlon
and Tory Gordon-Harris

How to discover more

Bugs is packed with creepy-crawlies and filled with great facts about them. By knowing a little bit about the way the book works, you will have fun reading and discover more.

Bug adventure

The book leads you on an exciting journey through the undergrowth and into the world of insects, spiders, and many other creepy-crawlies.

Find out what the biggest, slowest, and tastiest snails are in the facts and records box.

The introduction leads you into the slow world of slugs and snails.

The labels show you what the different parts of a snail are.

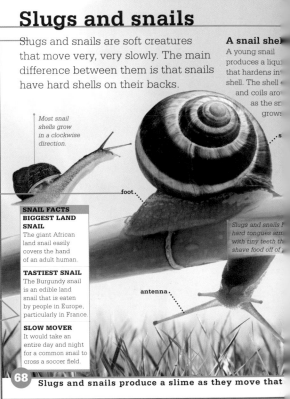

Slugs and snails

Slugs and snails are soft creatures that move very, very slowly. The main difference between them is that snails have hard shells on their backs.

A snail shell
A young snail produces a liqu that hardens int shell. The shell and coils aro as the sn grows

Most snail shells grow in a clockwise direction.

foot

Slugs and snails hard tongues att with tiny teeth th shave food off of

antenna

SNAIL FACTS

BIGGEST LAND SNAIL
The giant African land snail easily covers the hand of an adult human.

TASTIEST SNAIL
The Burgundy snail is an edible land snail that is eaten by people in Europe, particularly in France.

SLOW MOVER
It would take an entire day and night for a common snail to cross a soccer field.

68 Slugs and snails produce a slime as they move that

The Burgundy s is an edible land snail that is eaten by people in Europe particularly in Fran

SLOW MOVER
t would take a

Digital companion book

Download your free all-new digital book,

Bug Spotter

Log on to www.scholastic.com/discovermore

Enter your unique code: RCD3MGJFX7W6

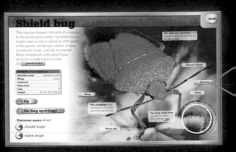

Packed with backyard bugs to spot

The caption provides a closer look at the lives of snails and slugs.

Small words focus on the bugs and give bite-size facts.

Look up a favorite subject in the contents.

Find out more
about how other bugs avoid danger on pages 28–31.

The long antenna has an eye on the end.

Snail eggs
The snails bury up to 100 eggs underground. When they hatch, the young snails eat their eggshells and climb up to the surface.

The short antenna is for feeling and smelling.

Breathing hole
Slugs and snails don't breathe through their mouths. Instead, they take in air through a hole in the sides of their bodies.

slug

breathing hole

Look out!
If a snail is under attack, it simply pulls its body into its shell and keeps still.

...otects the foot. The slime leaves silvery trails behind.

69

➤➤ **Find out more**
This takes you to another page to learn about other related facts.

The words along the bottom are questions or amazing facts.

Look up or learn new words in the glossary.

Look up a word in the index and find which page it's on.

Click the pop-ups for facts and stats

Encyclopedia entries to discover even more

Fun bug quizzes

Contents

Consultant: Kim Dennis-Bryan, PhD
Literacy Consultant: Barbara Russ,
21st Century Community Learning Center
Director for Winooski (Vermont) School District
Art Director: Bryn Walls
Designers: Clare Joyce, Ali Scrivens
Managing Editor: Miranda Smith
US Editor: Elizabeth Krych
Managing Production Editor:
Stephanie Engel
Cover Designers: Natalie Godwin,
Neal Cobourne
DTP: John Goldsmid
Visual Content Editor: Diane Allford-Trotman
**Executive Director of Photography,
Scholastic:** Steve Diamond

Library of Congress Cataloging-in-Publication
Data Available

ISBN 978-0-545-36574-1

10 9 8 7 6 5 4 3 2 1   12 13 14 15 16

Printed in Singapore   46
First edition, September 2012

Scholastic is constantly working to lessen the
environmental impact of our manufacturing
processes. To view our industry-leading
paper procurement policy, visit
www.scholastic.com/paperpolicy.

All about bugs

All about insects

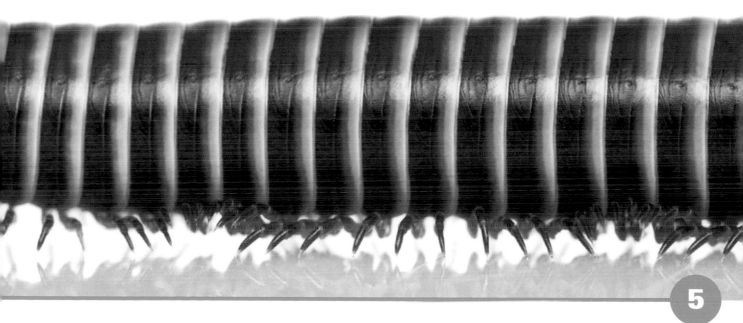

All about **bugs**

This Pandora sphinx moth caterpillar, red with white spots, is one of 160,000 species of moth found on Earth (see pages 37–39).

What is a bug?

Dig into the undergrowth and peek under logs, and you are bound to find the tiny, extraordinary creepy-crawlies of our world—commonly known as bugs.

No backbone

You have a backbone, just like all mammals, birds, reptiles, amphibians, fish, and birds do. A bug is an invertebrate, which means that it has no backbone.

weevil

No one knows how many bugs live on Earth. But we do

Sea bugs

Many invertebrates related to bugs live in the water, but this book looks only at land bugs.

This banded coral shrimp is a sea invertebrate.

97%
OF THE WORLD'S ANIMALS ARE **INVERTEBRATES.**

Bug history

Invertebrates have been alive on Earth for at least 500 million years—possibly for a lot longer. Bugs similar to these weevils were around before the dinosaurs.

A weevil has a hard shell on the outside of its body instead of bones inside of it.

▶▶ **Find out more** about bug skeletons on pages 12–13.

know that there are many kinds yet to be discovered!

Bug groups

Bugs can be divided into six groups, based on differences such as the number of legs they have. If you count a bug's legs, you can probably name its group.

The insect group includes many species, from beetles and bees to flies and ants.

Spiders are closely related to scorpions and ticks.

Centipedes have lots and lots of legs.

Insects

NUMBER OF SPECIES:
At least 1 million
LEGS:
6
WINGS:
Most have 2 pairs
DIET:
Some eat meat, some eat plants, and some eat both

Arachnids

NUMBER OF SPECIES:
Over 100,000
LEGS:
8
WINGS:
None
DIET:
Mostly other bugs, but some eat small animals, and one type of spider eats only plants

Centipedes and millipedes

NUMBER OF SPECIES:
About 13,000
LEGS:
Up to 750
WINGS:
None
DIET:
Centipedes are meat-eaters, while millipedes are plant-eaters

Bugs are very **important to life on Earth.**

Bugs

Just one type of insect is a true "bug" (see page 42), but all creepy-crawlies are often referred to as bugs.

Worms live underground and have no eyes.

Many snails live in the ocean, but this one lives on land.

Although wood lice live only on land, their relatives live near or in water.

Wood lice

NUMBER OF SPECIES:
About 3,000
LEGS:
14
WINGS:
None
DIET:
Dead leaves and other rotting plants

Segmented worms

NUMBER OF SPECIES:
About 3,000
LEGS:
None
WINGS:
None
DIET:
Plants and rotten matter

Land slugs and snails

NUMBER OF SPECIES:
About 24,000
LEGS:
None
WINGS:
None
DIET:
Mostly plants, but a few species are meat-eaters

Many recycle dead matter and help new plants grow.

Bug skeletons

You have a skeleton inside your body, but a bug doesn't. Most bugs have hard skeletons on the outsides of their bodies.

A hard shell

Insects, spiders, centipedes, and wood lice have exoskeletons, or hard shells. Their soft body parts are inside.

The hard shell protects the bug from bumps and bangs.

rhinoceros beetle

The exoskeleton makes it difficult for hungry predators to eat the bug.

Moving joints

Bugs have soft joints between their legs and body parts, which means that they can bend in order to move.

praying mantis

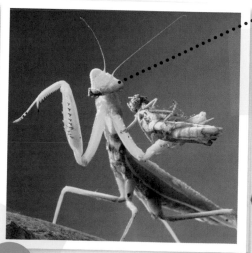

▶▶ **Find out more**
about beetles on
page 43.

*This shell's brown
color helps the
beetle hide in the
undergrowth.*

Growing and molting

1 Tight squeeze

Exoskeletons can't grow,
so this young spider has
to molt, or squeeze out of,
the one it was born with.

2 Stretching out

The spider stretches
its legs, and after just
a few hours its new
exoskeleton hardens.

Snail shells

A snail's hard shell doesn't cover
its body. Instead, it sits on top.

*A snail's shell
grows as the
snail grows.*

13

Hall of fame

There are loud ones, smelly ones, and some very strange-looking ones. Meet some of the record holders of the bug world.

SHORTEST ADULT LIFE
One kind of mayfly lives for only five minutes as an adult!

SMALLEST BUG
The tiny fairyfly is no bigger than this period.

MOST PAINFUL STING
The sting of the bullet ant causes a burning pain that lasts for 24 hours!

MOST LEGS
One type of millipede has 750 legs! That's more than any other animal in the world.

MOST INCREDIBLE JOURNEY
In autumn, monarch butterflies fly from the northern United States to Mexico to hibernate.

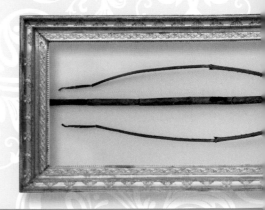

There are more record holders throughout this book.

STINKIEST BUG
If a stinkbug is disturbed, it releases nasty-smelling liquid.

HEAVIEST INSECT
The giant weta is as heavy as a small bird!

LONGEST HEAD
The giraffe-necked weevil has a huge neck compared to its body.

LONGEST INSECT
This stick insect, at 22 inches (55 cm) long, is longer than this open book is wide.

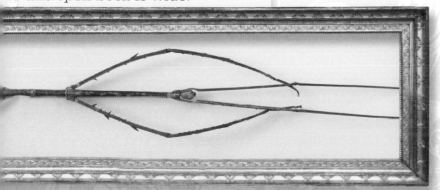

LOUDEST BUG ON LAND
The click of some cicadas is as loud as a chain saw.

Turn the page to meet the deadliest bug.

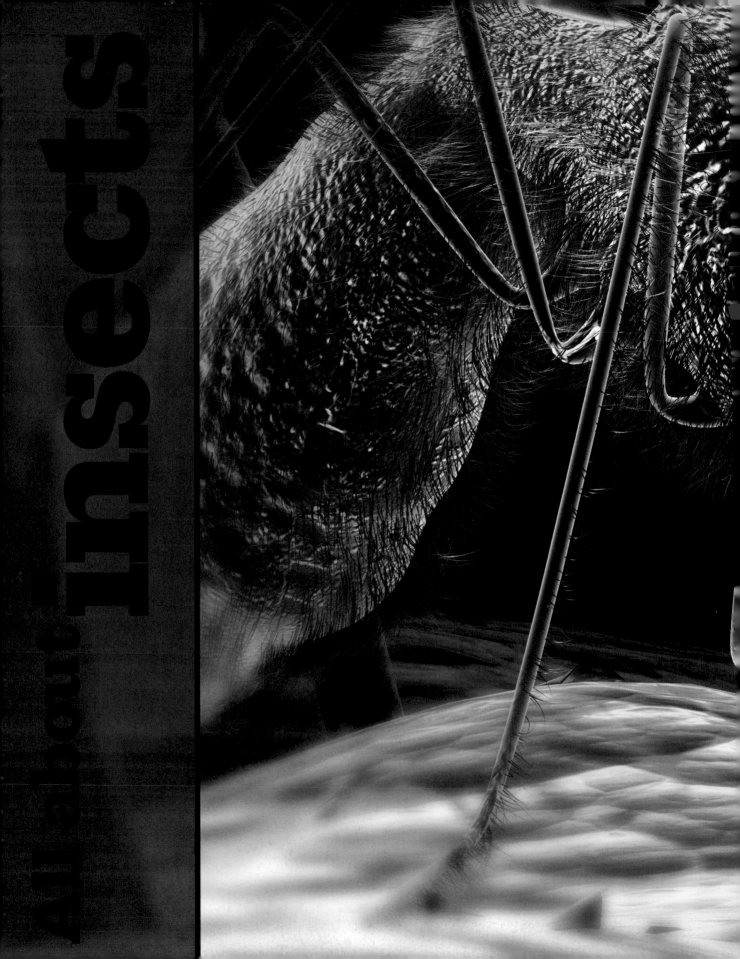

All about Insects

Mosquitoes are the deadliest insects. They feed mostly on plant juices and nectar, but some females also drink animal and human blood, spreading diseases. This female is piercing skin to suck up the blood beneath it.

Insects

You can spot an insect easily if it stays still—but it often doesn't! All insects have a few things in common that will help you identify them.

Count the legs

An adult insect has six legs. If a bug has any more or any fewer, it is not an insect. Count carefully!

The head is the top of three body parts. It includes antennae, eyes, and mouthparts.

head.

wasp.

The legs and wings are attached to the middle part of the body, the thorax.

thorax

abdomen

The abdomen holds the insect's heart and other organs.

INSECT FACTS

WEIRD FACT
Crickets hear through their knees!

COLDEST INSECT
The Weddell seal louse lives on seals that make their home in Antarctica.

WORST VENOM
The harvester ant has the most toxic venom of all insects.

BEST JUMPER
A cat flea can jump 100 times its own height.

Some insect babies look very different from their

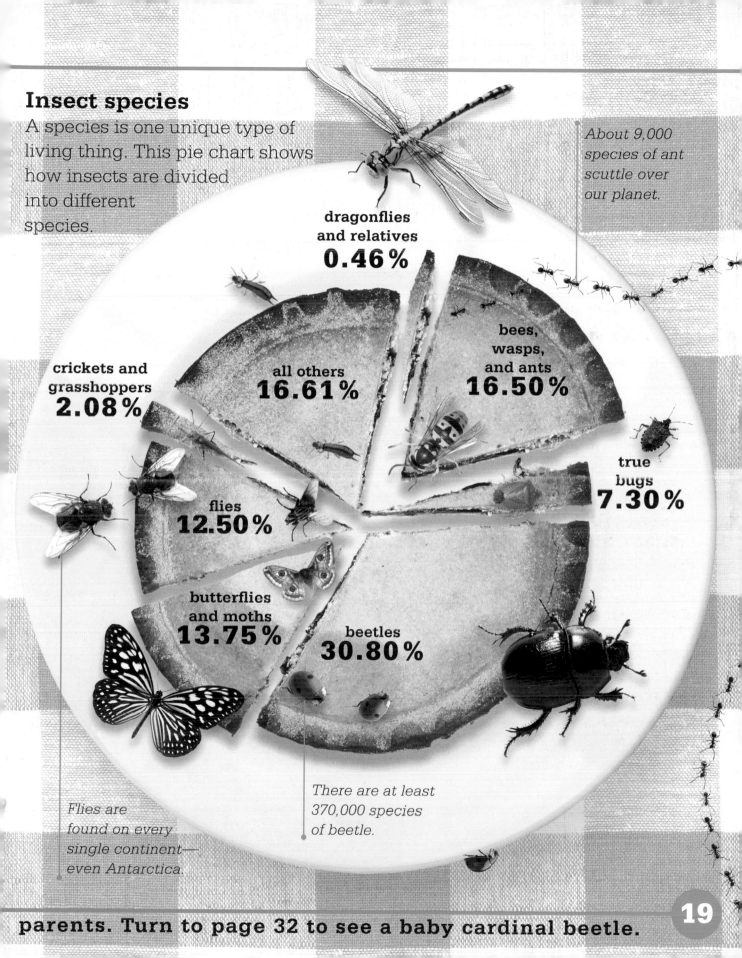

Insect species

A species is one unique type of living thing. This pie chart shows how insects are divided into different species.

About 9,000 species of ant scuttle over our planet.

dragonflies and relatives
0.46%

crickets and grasshoppers
2.08%

all others
16.61%

bees, wasps, and ants
16.50%

true bugs
7.30%

flies
12.50%

butterflies and moths
13.75%

beetles
30.80%

Flies are found on every single continent—even Antarctica.

There are at least 370,000 species of beetle.

parents. Turn to page 32 to see a baby cardinal beetle.

An insect collection

They all have three body parts and six legs, but insects come in an amazing range of shapes and colors.

great green bush cricket

South American cockroach

greenbottle fly

yellow ladybug

lychee stinkbug

rose chafer

tiger moth

thorn treehopper

winged swarmer termite

subterranean termite

Arizona turtle ant

European hornet

May bug

Pygopleurus vulpes

desert locust

honeypot ant

ground beetle

Schoenherr's blue weevil

East Africa flower beetle

smooth dor beetle

red cardinal beetle

sloe bug

fruit fly

Hercules beetle

snakefly

earwig

hornet mimic hoverfly

fire ant

hawthorn shield bug

red weaver ant

tooth-nosed snout weevil

jewel wasp

carpenter ant

lesser stag beetle

German wasp

horse ant

leaf-cutter ant

red and black striped shield bug

ak grasshopper

pale giant horsefly

southern green stinkbug

Taiwan spotted tiger beetle

hazel leaf-roller weevil

mayfly

brimstone moth

flower chafer

linden burncow bug

red and black froghopper beetle

praying mantis

polypore fungus beetle

Goliath beetle

harlequin bug

red-banded leafhopper

Westwood's leaf insect

cream-spot ladybug

mosquito

two-spotted ladybug

common housefly

fungus beetle

sharpshooter leafhopper

brown damselfly

false ladybug

teddy bear bee

hoverfly

green tiger beetle

dung beetle

mimusop stem borer beetle

bumblebee

oil beetle

frog-legged leaf beetle

Jamaican field cricket

grasshopper

green darner

European honeybee

leaf insect

giant water bug

three-lined potato beetle

American cockroach

human flea

stick insect

eastern tiger swallowtail butterfly

Wings

Insects are the only bugs that have wings, although not all insects have them. Flying is a great way to get around or to escape danger.

beetle

Two pairs

Flying insects have two pairs of wings, which they use in many ways.

Flight Insects can use their wings in these four different ways.

1 Darting wings

A lacewing moves its fore and hind wings independently, helping it change direction quickly.

lacewing

The veins, or lines, on each thin wing strengthen it and keep it from tearing in the air.

2 Flapping wings

A butterfly's front wings hook on to its back wings, so they move together in a slow flap.

butterfly

3 Steering sticks

A fly flies using one pair of wings. The other wings, called halteres, are used for steering.

housefly

Ants have wings only when they become adults. They fly

Quick wings

The hoverfly has one of the fastest wing flaps. It can beat its wings more than 1,000 times per second!

A ladybug holds its wing cases above its head when it flies.

ladybug

4 Wing cases

A beetle flies with one pair of wings. The other wings are hard cases that protect the flying wings when not in use.

Speedy flier

Hawk moths are among the fastest fliers in the insect world. They fly at a rate of 15 mph (24 kph).

to a new home, then tear their wings off.

Creepers and leapers

Insects are very good at getting around on the ground. How they move often depends on obstacles, what they like to eat, or if they are being chased.

Speedy sprinter

Many bugs are good runners. This tiger beetle is the fastest bug on Earth, able to run at 5.6 mph (9 kph). Its long legs and speed help it catch other insects.

meadow grasshopper

A grasshopper can jump 20 times its body length.

Leg power

If a grasshopper is disturbed, it uses its powerful back legs to launch itself into the air. Its back legs are longer and stronger than its other legs.

Jumper

The flea is the high jumper of the bug world. It has springs in its legs that enable it to jump 100 times its own height, up onto the furry animals that it lives on.

Walking on water

The water strider can walk across water. It stretches its legs wide, and tiny hairs on its feet help keep it from sinking.

Burrower

After a cicada hatches, the nymph (baby) burrows underground and lives there for 17 years!

Find out more about caterpillars on pages 34–35.

Creeper

Caterpillars use some of their 4,000 body muscles (humans only have about 700 muscles) to slide themselves along. They have short, clawed legs that grip leaves.

This caterpillar uses looping and stretching movements to creep along.

Some grasshoppers can walk, jump, and even fly!

Feeding time

While some insects are busy eating plants, others are just as busy eating one another!

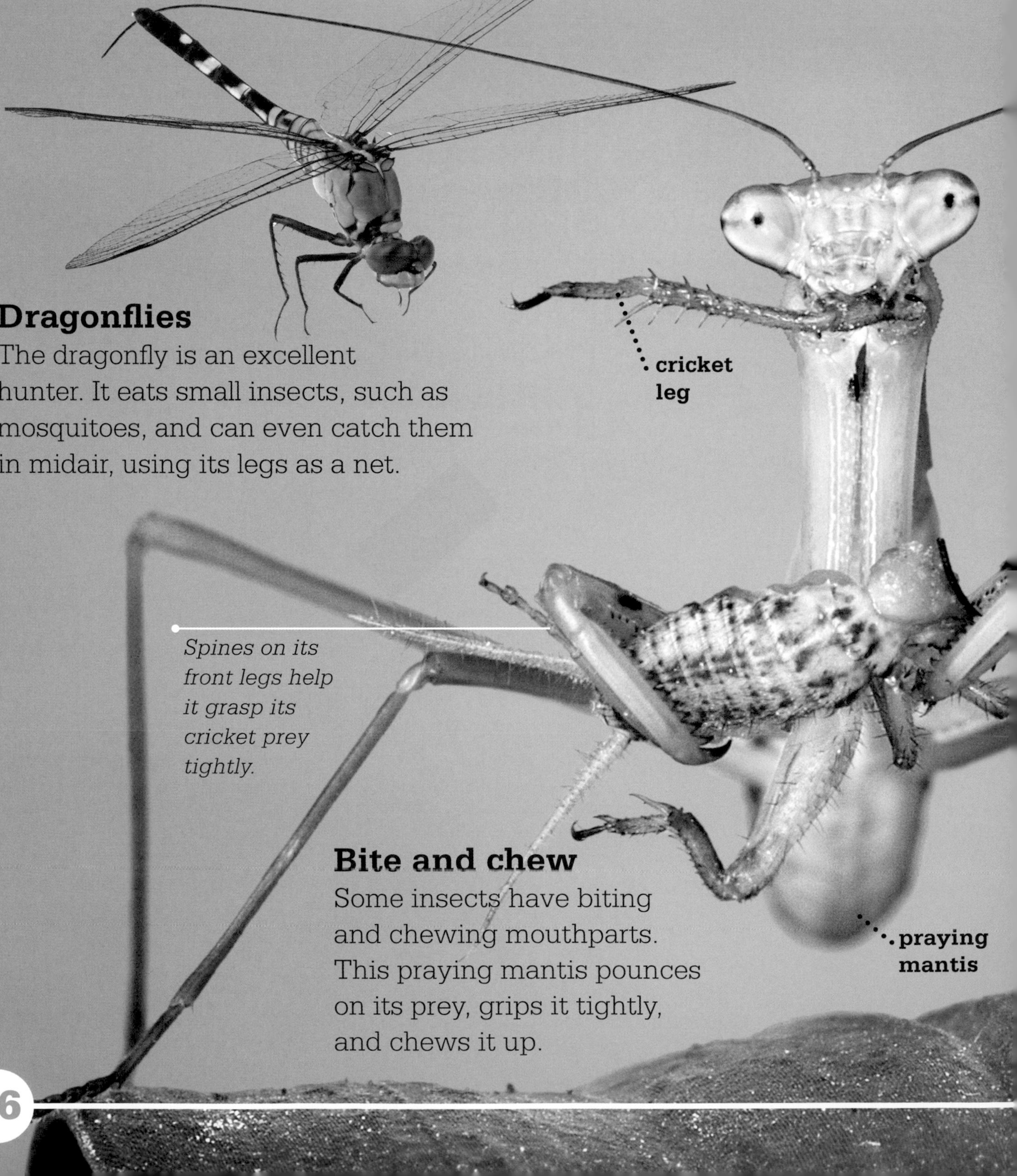

Dragonflies

The dragonfly is an excellent hunter. It eats small insects, such as mosquitoes, and can even catch them in midair, using its legs as a net.

cricket leg

Spines on its front legs help it grasp its cricket prey tightly.

Bite and chew

Some insects have biting and chewing mouthparts. This praying mantis pounces on its prey, grips it tightly, and chews it up.

praying mantis

Robber flies

A robber fly injects saliva and venom into its prey using its mouthparts, turning it to liquid. Then the insides can be sucked up.

Leaf-eaters

About 5 percent of all plants on Earth are eaten by insects, such as these sawfly wasp larvae.

Cupboard critters

Clothes moths' larvae eat fabric, such as wool and cotton. They love to nibble holes in your wool sweaters!

A butterfly coils up its proboscis when it isn't drinking.

A praying mantis can sit still for hours, waiting for prey to approach.

▶▶▶ **Find out more** about butterflies on pages 34–36.

Long proboscis

Many insects have piercing and sucking mouthparts. This butterfly has a long mouthpart, or proboscis, with which it sucks up flower nectar.

Defense

Insects have a lot of predators. Many animals eat them, other bugs eat them, and there are even plants that eat them. Some insects have built-in ways to avoid becoming lunch.

What's that?

Bird poop
This caterpillar looks like a bird dropping. Nothing will want to eat that!

Disguise
One way to keep from being eaten is to look like something else. Some mantises look just like orchid flowers. This camouflage also keeps them hidden from their prey.

This orchid mantis is white, like the white orchid next to it. Some mantises are pink, to match pink orchids.

Turn the page to see how one insect uses its color and

Here are some other clever disguises.

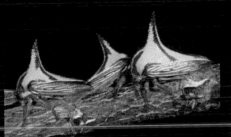

Stick

Stick insects look just like twigs. A predator can spot them only when they move.

Thorns

When these thorn bugs gather together, they look just like sharp thorns on a twig.

Scary eyes

Peanut head bugs open their wings to reveal large fake "eyes," which scare predators.

stick insect .·˙

This puss moth caterpillar rears its red head with fake black eyes to warn predators that it tastes bad.

Poison

Some bugs taste bad or are even poisonous. They often have bright colors to warn predators to stay away.

pattern to perfectly camouflage itself.

Can you see me?

The katydid's color and markings perfectly camouflage

Out of sight

At first glance, it appears that there is nothing but some moss on these pages. But look very carefully and you will see a katydid, which lives in the rainforests of Costa Rica, in Central America.

it in the moss, making it almost invisible to predators.

Amazing eggs

One thing insects are very, very good at is making more insects. Most lay eggs, and many lay a LOT of eggs.

cardinal beetle larva

Laying eggs

Eggs are laid in many different places.

Water eggs

Mosquitoes lay their eggs on water. Their babies live underwater until they become adults.

Egg clusters

Many butterflies lay their eggs on leaves. The cabbage white butterfly lays up to 150 eggs.

Mobile home

This giant water bug carries its eggs around on its back until they have hatched.

How many eggs?

Insects can lay between 1 and 2,000 eggs in a day (find out which one lays 2,000 eggs on page 47!). A lacewing lays up to 200 eggs over a period of about 4 weeks.

Lacewings lay each egg on a hairlike stalk.

adult cardinal beetle

A first meal

Here, an insect called a parent bug has laid its eggs on a leaf. When the babies hatch, they will gobble up the leaf.

Is that my baby?

Some insects, like the cardinal beetle above, have babies that look different from their parents. They go through metamorphosis, like butterflies do (see pages 34–35).

eggs

hatchlings

shield bug mother

parent bug eggs

Good mom

The shield bug mother is unusual because she stays with her eggs, guarding them fiercely even after they hatch.

Aphids

Aphids are extraordinary because they have live young and only sometimes lay eggs!

baby aphid

Metamorphosis

1 Egg

A swallowtail butterfly starts life as an egg. A female butterfly lays the egg on a leaf. It takes about 8 to 10 days for the egg to hatch.

2 Hatching

A tiny caterpillar emerges from the egg and eats its own eggshell. It begins to eat the leaf that it is sitting on, and starts to grow.

5 Pupating

The caterpillar sheds its skin once more and becomes a pupa. Inside its chrysalis, or protective covering, an amazing change is taking place.

6 Emerging butterfly

After 2 to 24 weeks (depending on the time of year), the chrysalis starts to split and the butterfly climbs out. Its wings are folded against its body.

When a caterpillar makes the change to a butterfly, th

3 Shedding skin

The caterpillar eats and eats, and grows and grows. It has to molt, or shed, its skin several times when it bursts out of it.

4 Attaching itself

After about 6 to 7 weeks, the caterpillar finds a safe place. It uses strands of silk that it makes in its body to attach itself to a plant.

7 Drying wings

The butterfly spends several hours stretching its wings and waiting for them to dry and strengthen before it can fly.

8 Flying away

The adult butterfly is now ready to fly away. It finds a mate and starts the cycle all over again, with an egg laid on a leaf.

process is known as complete metamorphosis.

Butterfly or moth?

Can you tell the difference between a butterfly and a moth? Here are a few hints.

Cairns birdwing butterfly.

Butterflies tend to feed and flutter around during the day.

Bright colors

Most butterflies are brightly colored, which makes them easier to identify. Turn the page and see if you recognize any.

That's a butterfly!

Here are a few things to look out for to spot a butterfly.

When a butterfly rests, it holds its wings on top of its body.

A butterfly's body tends to be slimmer than a moth's.

A butterfly has thin antennae with little knobs on the ends.

The wings are made up of tiny overlapping scales.

Dull colors

Moths are generally less colorful than butterflies are. They tend to be browns and grays. This coloring helps camouflage them when they rest during the day.

Atlas moth ....

Moths like to feed and fly around at night.

That's a moth!

Look for these features if you are moth spotting.

When a moth rests, it stretches its wings flat out to the sides.

A moth's body is generally thicker and hairier than a butterfly's.

A moth usually has long, feathery antennae.

Butterflies and moths are the only insects with scaly wings.

Butterflies and moths

With stunning colors and delicate wings, these insects are some of the most beautiful creatures on Earth.

magpie moth

Indian leaf butterfly

Scotch Burnet moth

yellow pansy butterfly

doris longwing butterfly

Australian gypsy moth

clipper butterfly

red admiral butterfly

sunset morpho butterfly

pink-bellied moth

comet moth

Cairns birdwing butterfly

hummingbird moth

orange forester butterfly

tiger-striped longwing butterfly

swallowtail butterfly

elephant hawk moth

tree nymph butterfly

cydno longwing butterfly

imperial moth

bizarre looper moth

deep yellow Euchlaena moth

blue morpho butterfly

Asterope sapphira butterfly

peacock butterfly

mint moth

clouded yellow butterfly

common cruiser butterfly

small grass-yellow butterfly

white antenna wasp moth

Wallace's golden birdwing butterfly

orange mimic butterfly

owl butterfly

common blue butterfly

blue swallowtail butterfly

great orange-tip butterfly

luna moth

lime hawk moth

purple-spotted swallowtail butterfly

blue cracker butterfly

tailed jay butterfly

knapweed fritillary

green-banded Urania moth

Spanish moon moth

ny rajah butterfly

Io moth

monarch butterfly

eighty-eight butterfly

swordtail doctor butterfly

small tortoiseshell butterfly

morpho helena butterfly

rosy maple moth

zebra longwing butterfly

oleander hawk moth

Atlas moth

tiger moth

Queen Alexandra's birdwing butterfly

purple emperor butterfly

great Mormon butterfly

sunset moth

paradise birdwing butterfly

beautiful marbled noctuid moth

marcella daggerwing butterfly

scarlet Mormon butterfly

blue pansy butterfly

African leafwing butterfly

zebra swallowtail butterfly

Cleopatra butterfly

Australian geometrid moth

cecropia moth

Flies

Flies buzz around everywhere, even on Antarctica. They are like tiny robots, with super senses and expert flying skills.

The eyes are HUGE. A fly is much better than people are at seeing movement and light, and it can see in every direction.

The stubby antennae are used for smelling. A fly can smell a dead animal from several miles away.

The proboscis, or mouth, is like a sponge. A fly extends it, then vomits through it onto its food. This turns the food to liquid so that the fly can suck it up.

Why do flies buzz?

A housefly can beat its wings 200 times a second. The wings flap so fast that they make a buzzing sound.

The feet are used to taste! A fly can tell as soon as it lands if something is good to eat.

Houseflies can't bite, but they can spread germs to

The hairs are very sensitive. They can sense if something is moving nearby, like a flyswatter!

The wings beat so fast that a fly can take off straight up into the air.

The fast wing beats help a fly change direction incredibly quickly.

The hairs on the fleshy pads of its feet give a fly a sticky surface that allows it to walk up walls or across ceilings.

your food.

Bugs and beetles

Bugs and beetles look similar but are different kinds of insect. True bugs are scuttling across this page, and beetles are rushing off the facing page.

soldier bug

red spot assassin bug

western leaf-footed bug

water scorpion

Parapioxys planthopper

red cabbage bug

eastern bloodsucking conenose bug

parent bug

forest bug

dock leaf bug

cicada

water boatman

tarnished plant bug

western conifer seed bug

red assassin bug

alder spittlebug

green stinkbug

aphid

froghopper

bronze orange bug

thorn treehopper

European birch shield bug

white spot assassin bug

red-banded leafhopper

backswimmer

horehound shield bug

burrowing bug

water strider

two-striped spittlebug

sloe bug

tobacco whitefly

firebug

cotton stainer

brown marmorated stinkbug

Aradus flower bug

sharpshooter leafhopper

wheel bug

Scutiphora metallic shield bug

Pycanum shield bug

Calliphara metallic shield bug

lantern bug

True bugs

True bugs are a family that eats using piercing and sucking mouthparts. They can suck sap from plants—or the insides out of other insects!

This assassin bug uses its proboscis to pierce skin and suck blood.

Can you find a spotted, bright red firebug?

14-spotted ladybug

black vine weevil

capricorn beetle

carrion beetle

giraffe-necked weevil

harlequin ladybug

metallic wood-boring beetle

narrowed Lixus weevil

22-spotted ladybug

king stag beetle

blue ground beetle

red palm weevil

spotted cucumber beetle

eyed click beetle

apricot weevil

round-necked longhorn beetle

fleabane tortoise beetle

soft-winged flower beetle

flower longhorn beetle

Colorado potato beetle

June beetle

flower chafer

poplar leaf beetle

green tiger beetle

locust borer beetle

elderberry borer beetle

smooth dor beetle

ivory-marked beetle

earth-boring dung beetle

bee beetle

hairy fungus beetle

hazel leaf-roller beetle

blue weevil

pasture splendor beetle

dead-nettle leaf beetle

Morimus longhorn beetle

tailed net-winged beetle

forest caterpillar hunter beetle

musk beetle

violin beetle

reed beetle

5-spotted ladybug

reddish-brown stag beetle

hairy spider beetle

sun beetle

hister beetle

chestnut click beetle

Staphylinid rove beetle

oil beetle

elephant beetle

Beetles

Beetles are either plant-eaters or meat-eaters, but unlike true bugs, they always chew up their food with their biting mouthparts.

This tiger beetle munches caterpillars and other insects in its huge jaws.

How many ladybugs can you see? Are they all red?

DUNG ALERT!
Beetle saves Australia

Too much poop!

Two and a half centuries ago, there were no cows in Australia. When Europeans went to live there, they took cows with them, and today there are about 20 million. Each cow produces wet, smelly dung about 12 times a

Australia

day. Dung beetles are generally excellent at cleaning up dung. But the dung beetles in Australia were used to the dry pellets dropped by Australian animals, such as kangaroos, and couldn't cope with the wet cow dung. So, over hundreds of years, cows ruined huge areas of grassland with their smelly dung.

Kangaroo dung is more solid than cow dung is.

The dung beetles in Australia were used to cleaning up kangaroo dung.

Native Australian dung beetles don't like sloppy dung at all.

About 500,000 acres (200,000 ha) of grazing land are lost every year to cow dung

When cow dung is not cleaned up, it attracts flies. Cow dung can draw 250 buffalo flies in a single day,

The larvae of flesh flies can also feed on cow dung.

so if you multiply those flies by all the cow dung dropped, you'll find that 60 billion flies could hatch EVERY DAY!

The beetles roll the dung into a large ball and push it to their burrow.

Australia had a lot of cow dung, and a lot of flies. Between 1969 and 1984, 50 different species of dung beetle from Europe and Africa—the kinds that love wet cow dung— were flown in to solve the problem. Dung beetles use dung as a home for their eggs and as food. They roll the dung into balls and take it underground. Doing this disturbed the breeding ground of the buffalo flies. In the end, 26 species of dung beetle did an amazing job of cleaning up the continent of Australia. They are true insect heroes.

Termites

Termites are the builders of the insect world. They live in huge colonies, or families, and build enormous nests.

Soldier termites are larger than worker termites.

Termite nests

Termites' nests are made of chewed-up mud and their own poop. The rock-solid nests can be taller than a human.

Workers

A nest is made up of a queen, king, soldiers, and workers. Workers build the nest, gather food, and tend to the queen and the eggs.

termite worker

All soldiers and workers are blind. Termites

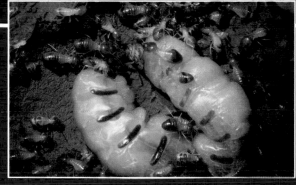

Termite queen

A termite queen is huge. She lives with a king, who is slightly smaller, and she lays all the eggs—some queens lay 2,000 a day!

ant

Termite soldiers

A termite nest has soldiers to guard it. Their job is to keep ants out of the nest, using their killer jaws.

termite soldier

Plant-eaters

Termites collect wood and plants, which they let rot inside their nests. They eat the rotten plants and also feed them to their babies.

communicate using smell and by tapping their heads.

Wasps

A buzz heard in the summer often means that there are wasps flying around. Watch out for their stingers!

antenna

Wasps

Many wasps are social, which means that they live in large groups. They work together to look after their young.

Solitary wasps

Some kinds of wasp live alone. They are called solitary wasps.

Laying eggs

Some solitary wasps find a fat caterpillar and lay eggs on its back.

Baby food

When the babies hatch, they eat the caterpillar!

.·. wasp
   nest

Paper nest

The queen paper wasp builds a nest out of a paperlike material made of chewed-up bark and saliva. She then lays a few eggs. When her offspring grow up, they continue building.

An egg is laid inside a cell. The eggs hatch into larvae, which pupate (see page 34) into adults.

·..... eye

Asian giant hornet eating a honeybee

Stings

Most wasps have stingers, which they use to defend themselves or to kill prey. The Asian giant hornet's sting has been known to kill a person.

Ants

Ants live together in huge colonies. There can be up to 8 million ants in one colony.

Cutting leaves

Leaf-cutter ants collect leaves, take them back to their underground nests, and use them to grow a fungus, which they eat.

Different jobs

Each ant has a specific job in its colony. This leaf-cutter ant has huge jaws to slice leaves into pieces.

The worker ants travel in long lines, each carrying leaf pieces.

Leaf-cutter nests are made up of underground rooms

More ants   Many species of ant have amazing skills.

Army ants

Army ants travel across jungle floors in colonies of millions. They eat any insect and can even kill a small mammal by working as a team to sting it to death.

Weaver ants

Weaver ants weave nests out of leaves. They use silk that their babies make to "stitch" the leaves together.

Wood ants

Wood ants live in big mound nests. They spray acid at anything that attacks them— even humans.

Carrying the load

A worker ant transports the leaf pieces. A leaf can be 20 times heavier than the ant. That's like you carrying a small car!

leaf-cutter ant

and tunnels that can stretch 16 feet (5 m) into the soil.

Honeypot ants

To make sure they always have food and drink, desert ants called honeypot ants store nectar in the bodies of certain ants in their colony, known as repletes.

Animals sometimes attack ant nests to eat the

Living lunchrooms

Worker ants collect nectar from flowers and food it to the repletes, whose bellies swell until they are huge. If the other ants run out of food, the repletes vomit up the nectar to feed the colony.

The repletes hang from the ceiling of the nest until they are needed.

honeypot ants. In Australia, even people eat them!

The life of a honeybee

A new nest
Honeybees live in huge colonies made up of workers and a queen. A new queen bee takes a group of workers and searches for a new place to nest.

The honeycomb
Young worker bees make honeycomb nests out of wax, which oozes from their bodies. They shape it into many small hexagonal (six-sided) cells.

Bee dance
In the spring, older bees collect pollen and nectar from flowers. Worker bees do special dances to show one another where the best flowers are.

Collecting pollen
Adult bees collect pollen to feed larvae and themselves. They carry it back to the nest in little pockets on their back legs.

People have used honeybee wax (beeswax) for

Laying eggs

Only the queen lays eggs. She lays one egg inside each cell. When an egg hatches into a larva, the workers feed it.

Worker bee

The larva pupates (see page 34), and an adult bee crawls out of the cell. The young bee helps repair the nest, and guards it by stinging predators.

Making honey

The bees also take nectar back to the nest in their stomachs. The nectar is turned into honey and stored in spare cells in the nest.

Delicious honey

The honey feeds the bees throughout the winter. All over the world, people keep beehives so that we can eat honey, too.

thousands of years. It is often used to make candles.

All about other bugs

Spiders are fierce hunters. In this picture, taken with an electron microscope, a garden spider paralyzes a fly by injecting venom through its fangs.

A collection of other bugs

Some of these bugs have many legs; some have no legs. But none have six legs, because none are insects.

green huntsman spider

St. Andrew's cross spider

ground spider

flat-backed millipede

goldenrod spider

European castor bean tick

ladybug spider

varroa mite

American dog tick

European garden spider

golden silk spider

velvet mite

raft spider

Spanish slug

daddy longlegs spider

house spider

ant mimic spider

deer tick

sac spider

yellow-spotted millipede

vinegaroon

pseudoscorpion

great black slug

common earthworm

Arthrosphaera pill millipede

spiny orb weaver spiders

pinworm

red slug

house centipede

giant African land snail

cucumber spider

Tanzanian tailless whip scorpion

leopard slug

emperor scorpion

common garden snail

Apheloria peach pit millipede

tiger centipede

giant blue earthworm

jumping spiders

common false widow spider

Sydney funnel-web spider

Ocala giant millipede

As you read the next pages, see if you can figure out

Mexican red-kneed tarantula

green lynx spider

white-lipped snail

Arizona bark scorpion

stretch spider

wasp spider

Usambara orange baboon tarantula

brown recluse spider

Diaea crab spider

slender crab spider

ghost slug

Madagascan Helicophanta snail

three varieties of wood louse

venusta orchard spider

brown-lipped snail

southern gloss crab spider

Solfugid sun spider

Pacific banana slug

redback spider

Goliath bird-eating spider

banded garden spider

cardinal spider

black widow spider

American giant millipede

Texas giant centipede

Kinabalu giant earthworm

door snail

red triangle slug

wolf spider

59

which groups these bugs belong to.

Arachnids

Spiders, scorpions, ticks, and mites are all related to one another. They are known as arachnids.

garden spider

crab spider

black widow spider

crab spider

golden orb weaver spider

cucumber spider

wasp spider

Mexican red-kneed tarantula

ARACHNID FACTS

DEADLIEST ARACHNID
A bite from a Brazilian wandering spider can kill a person.

BIGGEST SPIDER
The Goliath bird-eating spider is the size of a dinner plate.

BIGGEST WEB
Webs belonging to the Darwin's bark spider have been found that measure 80 feet (24 m) across.

Some insects look a lot like spiders, so count the legs

Other arachnids Here are some spider relatives.

Scorpion
A scorpion has massive claws, and a stinger at the end of its tail.

Whip scorpion
A tailless whip scorpion uses its extralong front legs to catch prey.

Mite
This red velvet mite is so tiny that it cannot easily be seen on the ground.

Arachnids
Arachnids always have eight legs and two body parts—a fused head and thorax, and an abdomen.

Meat-eaters
Arachnids are meat-eaters, so they must catch their prey to have a meal. They are all very good hunters.

carefully. If you can count eight, it's an arachnid.

Spiders

Spiders are carnivores, or meat-eaters, and are some of the greatest hunters of the bug world. They are a fly's biggest enemy.

The orb weaver spider uses a web to catch its prey. Most make a new web each day.

Spiderwebs

All spiders can make silk inside their bodies. Some use the silk to weave webs. When an insect flies into the web, it gets trapped.

This jumping spider has eight eyes! It uses all of them to hunt its prey.

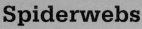

Venom

Spiders eat most other bugs. They don't have teeth, but they have sharp fangs filled with venom that they use to kill their prey.

A jumping spider doesn't use a web to catch its prey. It can leap and attack it.

fly

Find out more about flies on pages 40–41.

This mother wolf spider carries her egg sac around with her.

Silk spinning Spiders spin silk for many purposes.

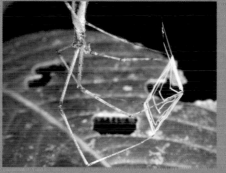

Silk trap
This spider is making a sticky silk to wrap up its prey.

Web net
This net-casting spider makes a little net that it drops onto its prey.

Egg sac
This spider has wrapped its eggs in a silky ball to keep them safe.

An orb weaver spider can spin a web in just one hour.

63

Centipede or millipede?

It's easy to spot centipedes and millipedes, because they both have lots of legs. But can you tell which is which?

giant millipede

tiger centipede

Centipedes

A centipede has fewer legs than a millipede does—it has one pair of legs on each body segment. It is an aggressive meat-eater and can run fast.

giant African millipede

CENTIPEDE AND MILLIPEDE FACTS

BIGGEST CENTIPEDE

The Amazonian giant centipede is the largest, reaching over 1 foot (30 cm) in length.

LONGEST MILLIPEDE

The longest giant millipede alive today is 10 inches (25 cm).

WEIRD FACT

300 million years ago, centipedes grew to over 3 feet (1 m) long.

Millipedes

A millipede has two pairs of legs on each body segment and moves quite slowly. It is a gentle plant-eater.

A millipede munches plants as it moves through undergrowth.

Wood lice live everywhere except for polar regions

Wood lice

Wood lice are different from their relatives, which all live in or near water. Wood lice are the only crustaceans that live only on land.

Drop and roll!
If they get scared, some wood lice can roll their bodies into tight balls.

Wood lice are related to lobsters and crabs.

All wood lice have 14 legs.

A damp home
Roll over a dead log in a damp place and you will often find wood lice. They eat dead organic matter that includes plants and other bugs.

WOOD LOUSE FACTS

EGG FACT
Wood louse babies have to hatch in water. The mother has a pouch under her abdomen that is filled with fluid. The young hatch and absorb some of the moisture before leaving the pouch.

BIGGEST WOOD LOUSE
Some wood lice can grow to over 1 inch (3 cm) long.

common rough wood louse

and deserts.

Earthworms

They may be small and live underground, but worms do a very important job for our world: They help keep soil healthy.

Burrowing worms

Earthworms have no legs, wings, or eyes, but they can sense light and feel heat. If they get near the surface, they know to burrow back down.

The slightly bigger part of a worm's body is called the saddle. It is nearer the head.

earthworm

Watch out, worm!

Worms have tiny bristles, like little hairs, on their bodies. When a bird tries to tug a worm out of the ground, it grips the soil with its bristles. Sometimes the worm wins; sometimes the bird wins!

Soil is full of worms. If you dug up a soccer field, you

Keeping soil rich Earthworms help improve soil in many ways.

Helping soil
Worms eat dead plants, turning them back into good soil as they poop.

Protecting soil
As worms move, they make air tunnels that keep the earth healthy.

Compost
Some people use worms to munch up their vegetable leftovers to make rich soil.

WORM FACTS

LONGEST EARTHWORM
The giant Gippsland earthworm can grow over 6.5 feet (2 m) in length.

LOTS OF HEART
An earthworm appears pink because its blood vessels are close to the surface of its skin. Blood is pumped around its body by a series of five arches, which are like hearts.

could easily find over 1 million earthworms.

Slugs and snails

Slugs and snails are soft creatures that move very, very slowly. The main difference between them is that snails have hard shells on their backs.

A snail shell

A young snail produces a liquid that hardens into a shell. The shell grows and coils around as the snail grows.

Most snail shells grow in a clockwise direction.

shell

foot

Slugs and snails have hard tongues armed with tiny teeth that shave food off plants.

antenna

SNAIL FACTS

BIGGEST LAND SNAIL

The giant African land snail easily covers the hand of an adult human.

TASTIEST SNAIL

The Burgundy snail is an edible land snail that is eaten by people in Europe, particularly in France.

SLOW MOVER

It would take an entire day and night for a common snail to cross a soccer field.

Slugs and snails produce a slime as they move that

Snail eggs

Some snails bury up to 100 eggs underground. When they hatch, the young snails eat their eggshells and climb up to the surface.

The long antenna has an eye on the end.

The short antenna is for feeling and smelling.

Find out more about how other bugs avoid danger on pages 28–31.

Look out!

If a snail is under attack, it simply pulls its body into its shell and keeps still.

Breathing hole

Slugs and snails don't breathe through their mouths. Instead, they take in air through a little hole in the sides of their bodies.

slug

breathing hole

protects the foot. The slime leaves silvery trails behind.

Pests and plagues

Many bugs are very useful to our world, but some kinds of bug can be very harmful indeed. Meet some bugs that are nasty pests or terrifying plagues.

The deadly mosquito

Female mosquitoes suck human blood, leaving itchy bumps. Some species can spread a deadly disease called malaria, which kills over a million people each year.

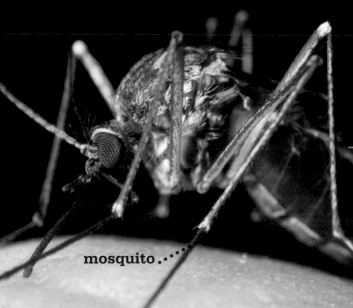

mosquito·····

Head lice can spread from person to person.

The mosquito is considered the most deadly animal in the world because malaria kills so many people.

Locust plague

Every so often in Africa, Asia, and Australia, usually if the weather changes quickly, the whole sky becomes dark. Millions of locusts swarm through the air, then land to eat huge amounts of crops.

A locust swarm is very harmful to farmers.

··········· **desert locust**

Head louse

The first sign of a head louse is an itchy head. The louse lays its eggs, called nits, on human hair, and when they hatch they drink blood from the scalp.

··· **head louse**

········· **human hair**

Colorado
potato
beetle ·

Colorado potato beetle

The Colorado potato beetle eats potato plants. It is a huge pest in the United States and can ruin whole fields of potatoes.

Bug heroes

If humans left Earth, life would continue as normal. But if bugs left, our planet would be a very different place. We depend on bugs more than you might think.

Bug food
Lots of animals eat bugs to survive, and that includes us! About 80 percent of the world's population eats insects.

aphid

ladybug

Pest control
Aphids eat plants that humans also like to eat, so farmers let ladybugs loose on their crops. The ladybugs gobble up the aphids and leave more food for us.

Farmers also use chemicals called pesticides to kill pests. But pesticides kill useful insects, too. So ladybugs are good for everyone!

Cleaning service

fly·····

Many types of bug help clean up Earth. If we didn't have bugs breaking down dead matter, there would be a lot of rotting mess lying around.

Flies

Flies often lay their eggs on dead animals. When the maggots hatch, they eat all the dead flesh.

Millipedes

Millipedes eat rotting leaves. They then poop the nutrients from them back into the soil.

Stag beetles

Stag beetle larvae eat the wood of dead trees, which helps clear land for new trees to grow.

The venom in this bee's stinger can be used to make medicine.

Pollinating bees

Bees are important because they spread pollen from flower to flower when they collect nectar. The pollen enables the flowers to make seeds.

Interview with an

Name: Dr. George McGavin
Profession: Entomologist (insect expert), explorer, and TV show host

Q ## When did you become interested in bugs?

A As a child I loved animals; then I realized that bugs were right on my doorstep. You don't need to travel anywhere to watch bugs—they are everywhere.

Q ## How did you become an entomologist?

A I studied zoology [animals] at Edinburgh University and the Natural History Museum in London [UK].

···**blue swallowtail butterfly**

Q ## What is your job like? Is it fun?

A I get to travel to rainforests, deserts, islands, and mountains, looking for and studying insects and filming them for TV. There are so many extraordinary bugs that do so many interesting things that they never get boring. I have the best job in the world!

entomologist

Q Have you ever eaten any insects?

A Yes, often. Many people in the world eat insects as part of their daily diet. They are very good for you, and some taste surprisingly good.

Q Are there any bugs that taste really bad?

A After the silk has been removed from the silk moth pupa, the Chinese boil up the pupae and eat them. To me, they taste absolutely awful.

Q If you had a bug restaurant, what would you put on the menu?

A Black African crickets fried in a little oil and garlic—delicious!

Q What is the most painful bite or sting you have received?

A Being bitten by a swarm of army ants was very, very painful. But the most painful single sting was from a scorpion.

Q Have you discovered any new insects?

A Yes, many. There are so many undiscovered species out there. That's what makes expeditions so exciting. So far I have had an ant, a shield bug, a planthopper, and a cockroach named after me.

Q Do you have any favorite bugs?

A I love them all! But if I had to pick one species then I would say bees, because they are so important to our world. Without bees helping to pollinate them, many plants would die out completely.

......**horsehead grasshopper**

Glossary

abdomen
The part of an animal that contains its heart and other organs.

antenna
One of the two sticklike feelers on an insect's head that it uses to sense the world around it. The plural of *antenna* is *antennae*.

arachnid
An invertebrate with eight legs and two body sections. Spiders and scorpions are arachnids.

camouflage
Natural coloring that helps animals blend in with their surroundings.

carnivore
An animal that eats meat.

cell
A small room in a nest or honeycomb, used as a home for a baby bee or wasp or to store honey.

colony
A large group of the same kind of animal living together.

compost
Rotting plants that are used to nourish the soil.

crustacean
An animal that has a hard shell. Wood lice are the only crustaceans that live on land.

entomologist
A scientist who studies insects.

exoskeleton
The hard outer shell that protects the bodies of many invertebrates.

haltere
One of the pair of small wings that a fly uses to steer while flying.

head
The top part of an animal, which includes its eyes and mouth.

insect
A land invertebrate with three body sections, six legs, and often two pairs of wings.

invertebrate
An animal with no backbone and often an exoskeleton, or hard outer shell.

larva
An insect in the second stage of its life, after it hatches from an egg and before it is an adult. The plural of *larva* is *larvae*.

metamorphosis
The series of physical changes that an animal such as a butterfly goes through as it becomes an adult.

molt
To shed an outgrown body part, such as an exoskeleton.

nectar
A sweet liquid, made by flowers, that some bugs eat and that bees make into honey.

plague
A widespread disaster often caused by the invasion of insects such as locusts.

predator
An animal that hunts and eats other animals.

prey
An animal that is hunted and eaten by another animal.

proboscis
The long mouthparts of an animal such as a butterfly.

pupa
An insect in the middle stage of its life, when it rests and changes into an adult. The plural of *pupa* is *pupae*. To pupate is to become a pupa or to be in this phase.

social
Living in groups.

species
A group of living things that look alike and can breed together.

spider
An invertebrate with eight legs and two body sections.

thorax
The middle part of an insect, which its legs and wings are attached to.

true bug
A type of insect with piercing mouthparts, four wings, and usually long antennae. Aphids, cicadas, and water bugs are true bugs.

venom
A poison that some animals use to kill their prey.

zoology
The study of animals.

Index

Moths always seem to flutter around lights at night. It may be because they use the Moon to guide their journeys, and our lights confuse them.

Thank you

Photography

1: Alex Wild; 4bl: Subbotina/Dreamstime; 4–5: Eric Isselée/iStockphoto; 6–7: Skip Moody – Rainbow/Getty; 8–9: Igor Siwanowicz; 9tl: worldswildlifewonders/Shutterstock; 10 (spiderweb): Hemera/Thinkstock; 10 (spider on web): Thinkstock; 10 (butterfly): Dreamstime; 10 (spider, centipede): iStockphoto; 10 (ladybug): Dreamstime; 10 (beetle): iStockphoto; 10 (scorpion, millipede): Dreamstime; 11 (ants, l to r): iStockphoto, iStockphoto, Dreamstime, Dreamstime, Dreamstime; 11 (worm on finger): iStockphoto; 11 (t wood louse, c worm, large snail): Dreamstime; 11 (l wood louse, r wood louse): iStockphoto; 11 (b wood louse, b worm, r snail, b snail): Dreamstime; 12bl: Kristina Postnikova/Shutterstock; 12–13: Alex Wild; 13tc, 13tr: Cathy Keifer/Shutterstock; 13br: mike_expert/iStockphoto; 14–15 (background): AnastasiaSonne/Shutterstock; 14–15 (all frames): Iakov Filimonov/Shutterstock; 14 (fairyfly): George Poinar Jr. & John T. Huber/Wikipedia; 14 (bullet ant): Barbara Strnadova/Science Photo Library; 14 (mayfly): Stana/Shutterstock; 14 (millipede): Ocean/Corbis; 14 (butterfly): Jordan McCullough/iStockphoto; 14 (map): Vladislav Gurfinkel/Shutterstock; 14–15 (stick insect): Natural History Museum, London/Science Photo Library; 15 (giant weta): Thierry Berrod, Mona Lisa Production/Science Photo Library; 15 (stinkbug): Steve Heap/Shutterstock; 15 (giraffe-necked weevil): kurt_G/Shutterstock/Shutterstock; 15 (cicada): Caleb Foster/Shutterstock; 16–17: 3D4Medical/Photo Researchers, Inc.; 18l: Scholastic; 18r: irin-k/Shutterstock; 19 (pie): Chris Leachman/Shutterstock; 19 (dragonfly): Hintau Aliaksei/Shutterstock; 19 (ants): asharkyu/Shutterstock; 19 (wasp): irin-k/Shutterstock; 19 (stinkbug): Melinda Fawver/Shutterstock; 19 (green bug): Alex Kuzovlev/Shutterstock; 19 (dung beetle): Kletr/Shutterstock; 19 (ladybug): Scholastic; 19 (butterfly): Eric Isselée/Shutterstock; 19 (moth): Henrik Larsson/Shutterstock; 19 (large fly): irin-k/Shutterstock; 19 (red-eyed fly): Le Do/Shutterstock; 19 (grasshopper): Route66/Shutterstock; 19 (earwig): Cre8tive Images/Shutterstock; 20 (thorn treehopper): Francesco Tomasinelli/Photo Researchers, Inc.; 20 (honeypot ant): ANT Photo Library/Photo Researchers, Inc.; 20 (Arizona turtle ant): Alex Wild; 20 (leaf-cutter ant): Mark Bowler/Photo Researchers, Inc.; 20–21 (all others): Dreamstime, iStockphoto, Thinkstock; 22t: Ian Wilson/Shutterstock; 22bl: Peter Waters/Shutterstock; 22bc: Marco Uliana/Shutterstock; 22br: irin-k/Shutterstock; 22–23 (ladybug in flight): A & J Visage/Alamy; 22–23 (grass): Yellowj/Shutterstock; 23tl: Ian Grainger/Getty; 23br: Getty; 24tl: Dreamstime; 24cl, 24cr: Photoshot Holdings Ltd/Alamy; 24–25c: Alex Fieldhouse/Alamy; 25tl: coopder1/iStockphoto; 25tc: Dreamstime; 25tr: iStockphoto; 25bl: Ziga Camernik/Shutterstock; 25bc: Credit: Ioannis Pantzi/Shutterstock; 25br: Ziga Camernik/Shutterstock; 26tl: Dreamstime; 26–27: Cathy Keifer/Shutterstock; 27tl: Atarel/Dreamstime; 27tc: Paulbroad/Dreamstime; 27tr: Guido Gerding/Wikipedia; 27c: PHOTOTAKE Inc./Alamy; 27br: Dave Marsden/Alamy; 28–29b: Igor Siwanowicz; 28tr: Tonnywu76/Dreamstime; 29tl: Tom Brakefield/Thinkstock; 29tc: Gary Retherford/Photo Researchers, Inc.; 29tr: dra_schwartz/iStockphoto; 29br: Gumenuk Vitalij/Dreamstime; 30–31: Thomas Marent/Visuals Unli44mited/Corbis; 32tr: Henrikhl/Dreamstime; 32cl: Antonio Perez Devesa/Dreamstime; 32cm: Power and Syred/Photo Researchers, Inc.; 32cr, 32bl: Alex Wild; 33tl: Mille19/Dreamstime; 33tc (leaves): shumelki/iStockphoto; 33tr (eggs on leaf): Duncan McEwan/NPL; 33cl: Wong Hock Weng/Alamy; 33b: Alex Wild; 34 (all): Thomas Marent; 35tl: Buquet Christophe/Shutterstock; 35tr, 35bl, 35br: Thomas Marent; 36 (background): Smit/Shutterstock; 36l: Dreamstime; 36 (magnifying glass): Andreas Rodriguez/iStockphoto; 36 (scales): Natural History Museum, London/Science Photo Library; 36brt: Lisa Thornberg/iStockphoto; 36brc: Antagain/iStockphoto; 36brb: Willmetts/Dreamstime; 37tr: Bthompso2001/Dreamstime; 37cr: Antagain/iStockphoto; 37blt: Charles Brutlag/iStockphoto; 37blc: PeterWaters/Dreamstime; 37blb: Tonnywu76/Dreamstime; 39 (Queen Alexandra's birdwing butterfly): dieKleinert/Alamy; 39 (Spanish moon moth): Ray Coleman/Photo Researchers, Inc.; 38–39 (all others): Dreamstime, iStockphoto, Thinkstock; 40–41: Nathan Griffith/Corbis; 42 (tarnished plant bug): Alex Wild; 42 (water boatman): James Lindsey at Ecology of Commanster/Wikipedia; 42 (alder spittlebug): Ettore Balocchi/Wikipedia; 42 (thorn treehopper): Francesco Tomasinelli/Photo Researchers, Inc.; 42 (bronze orange bug): Jan Anderson/Wikipedia; 42 (two-striped spittlebug, wheel bug): Kaldari/Wikipedia; 42 (Scutiphora metallic shield bug): Benjamint444/Wikipedia; 42 (soldier bug): Ettore Balocchi/Wikipedia; 42 (western leaf-footed bug): Alex Wild; 42 (Parapioxys planthopper): Slashme/

Wikipedia; 42 (eastern bloodsucking conenose bug): Alex Wild; 42 (parent bug): Evanherk/Wikipedia; 42 (horehound shield bug): Olei/Wikipedia; 42 (backswimmer): Wikipedia; 42 (forest bug): Darkone/Wikipedia; 42 (assassin bug with proboscis): David Scharf/Photo Researchers, Inc.; 43 (tiger beetle with jaws): Ted Kinsman/Photo Researchers, Inc.; 42–43 (all others): Dreamstime, iStockphoto, Thinkstock; 44tc: Alfonso de Tomas/Shutterstock; 44bl: Dirk Freder/iStockphoto; 44bc: Robynmac/Dreamstime; 44br: Sherj/Dreamstime; 45tr: Richard Goerg/iStockphoto; 45 (flies): NatureOnline/Alamy; 45 (larvae): Goruppa/Dreamstime; 45b: Cooper5022/Dreamstime; 46tc: Alex Wild; 46tr: iStockphoto; 46c: Dreamstime; 46–47b: Eye of Science/Photo Researchers, Inc.; 47tl: Dreamstime; 47tr: Photoshot Holdings Ltd/Alamy; 48tr: Jocic/Dreamstime; 48bl: iStockphoto; 48bc: Dreamstime; 48–49c: Visuals Unlimited/Corbis; 49tl: iStockphoto; 49tr: Dreamstime; 49c: Jens Ottoson/Shutterstock; 49br: Scott Camazine/Photo Researchers, Inc.; 50tl, 50cl: Alex Wild; 50bl: Eric Isselée/Shutterstock; 50br: Eric Isselée/iStockphoto; 51tl: Christian Ziegler/Minden Pictures; 51tc: Hugh Lansdown/Shutterstock; 51tr: Warren Photographic; 51bl: Dreamstime; 51br: Eric Isselée/Shutterstock; 52–53: Reg Morrison/Auscape/Minden Pictures; 54tl, 54tr: Thomas Marent; 54bl, 54br: Dreamstime; 55tl: Alex Wild; 55tr: Dreamstime; 55bl: Scott Camazine/Photo Researchers, Inc.; 55br: iStockphoto; 55 (honeypot): Dreamstime; 56–57: Volker Steger/Photo Researchers, Inc.; 58 (Arthrosphaera pill millipede): L. Shyamal/Wikipedia; 58 (Tanzanian tailless whip scorpion): Ivan Kuzmin/Shutterstock; 58 (Apheloria peach pit millipede): Bob Walker/Wikipedia; 58 (giant blue earthworm): Fletcher & Baylis/Photo Researchers, Inc.; 58 (jumping spider l): Alex Wild; 58 (Sydney funnel-web spider): James van den Broek/Shutterstock; 58 (varroa mite): Alex Wild; 58 (flat-backed millipede): Rob and Stephanie Levy/Wikipedia; 58 (yellow-spotted millipede): Rowland Shelley/Wikipedia; 59 (Madagascan Helicophanta snail): Jjargoud/Wikipedia; 59 (white-lipped snail): Mad Max/Wikipedia; 59 (Arizona bark scorpion): Alex Wild; 59 (ghost slug): AmGueddfa Cymru/National Museum of Wales/Wikipedia; 59 (Goliath bird-eating spider): Barbara Strnadova/Photo Researchers, Inc.; 59 (Solfugid sun spider): Alex Wild; 59 (red triangle slug): Ros Runciman/Wikipedia; 59 (Kinabalu giant earthworm): SuperStock; 59 (door snail): Andrew Dunn/andrewdunnphoto.com/Wikipedia; 58–59 (all others): Dreamstime, iStockphoto, Thinkstock; 60 (web, golden orb weaver spider, garden spider): Thinkstock; 60 (crab spider 1): Dreamstime; 60 (cucumber spider): Thinkstock; 60 (crab spider r, wasp spider): Dreamstime; 60 (black widow spider): Thinkstock; 60–61b: Natural History Museum, London/Photo Researchers, Inc.; 61tl, 61tc, 61tr: Dreamstime; 62tr: Brandon Alms/iStockphoto; 62cl: Dreamstime; 62b: D. Kucharski & K. Kucharska/Shutterstock; 63t: Igor Siwanowicz; 63bl: Dreamstime; 63bc: Dr Morley Read/Photo Researchers, Inc.; 63br: Dreamstime; 64tl: fivespots/Shutterstock; 64cl: Eric Isselée/Shutterstock; 64c: Ocean/Corbis; 64r: Paul Taylor/Getty; 65trl, 65trc: Chris Howey/Shutterstock; 65trr: Santia/Shutterstock; 65c: Thomas Payne/Shutterstock; 65cr, 65bc: Chris Howey/Shutterstock; 65br: Robert Harding World Imagery/Getty; 66tl, 66tr: Dreamstime; 66b: FLPA/Alamy; 67tl: Jacana/Photo Researchers, Inc.; 67tc, 67tr: Dreamstime; 67b: Nigel Cattlin/Alamy; 67 (worm on finger): iStockphoto; 68–69 (background): Yellowj/Shutterstock; 68cl: Dreamstime; 68–69c: blackpixel/Shutterstock; 69tl: Juniors Bildarchiv/Alamy; 69tr: aboikis/Shutterstock; 69cr: Thinkstock; 69b: Eric Isselée/Shutterstock; 70–71 (background): Photoshot/Alamy; 70bl: Henrik Larsson/Shutterstock; 70–71c: Thierry Berrod, Mona Lisa Production/Photo Researchers, Inc.; 71tr: Eric Isselée/Shutterstock; 71bc: Ivaschenko Roman/Shutterstock; 72–73 (background): Yellowj/Shutterstock; 72tr: iStockphoto; 72c: Courtesy of Crown, copyright FERA/Photo Researchers, Inc.; 73tr: Dreamstime; 73cl: Dreamstime; 73cm, 73cr, 73bl, 73br: Dreamstime; 74tr: Tim Martin; 74–75b: Dreamstime; 75: Alex Wild; 76bc, 76–77b: Eric Isselée/Shutterstock; 77bc: Eric Isselée/iStockphoto; 78–79: Dr. John Brackenbury/Photo Researchers, Inc.

Cover

Background: iStockphoto. Front cover: (tl) Peter Ardito/Getty; (c) Alain Even/Getty; (c background) Fitzer/iStockphoto; (bl) Dr. Jeremy Burgess/Photo Researchers, Inc.; (br) contour99/iStockphoto. Spine: Cosmln/Dreamstime. Back cover: (tl) Dreamstime; (tcl) Dreamstime, iStockphoto, Thinkstock; (tcr) Liewwk/Dreamstime; (tr) 3D4Medical/Photo Researchers, Inc.; (computer monitor) Manaemedia/Dreamstime.